VALIDATED BLOGSPOT TEMPLATE
HTML5 Validator: Validator.w3.org

Released on 1 March 2014

Notes:

This following Blogspot template is not under validator.w3.org or other official sites. Since this template is designed and tested by http://tina-andrew.blogspot.com, All stuffs in related to this template is appointed to the blog.

We commit in our works and really want your feedback for futher improvement, e.g. SEO Blogspot Template for increasing Better Visibility in Search Engine. All modifications, distribution or commercial purposes in related to this template you have purchased legally are now your own business :D
If you have trouble in replacing it, please contact me at :
http://www.facebook.com/Dev7Cyber2012

Warning:
Everytime you **add new gadget** you should **remove** this following script and save the template again!~

<b:include name='quickedit'/>

Remember that, when this template is launched in internet, HTML5 is in Experimental Version. All changes in related to HTML5, please contact me on my facebook, I'm very pleased to help you

By Herman Nz. http://www.facebook.com/Dev7Cyber2012

Let's start now!

Replace your current Blog script with this following scripts:

```
<?xml version="1.0" encoding="UTF-8" ?>
<!DOCTYPE html>
<HTML class='v2' dir='ltr' xmlns='http://www.w3.org/1999/xhtml'>
&lt;head&gt;
 <meta charset='UTF-8'/>
 <meta content=" name='google-site-verification'/>
 <meta content=" name='msvalidate.01'/>
 <meta content=" name='alexaVerifyID'/>
 <meta content='blogger' name='generator'/>
 <link href='http://your-blog-URL-here.blogspot.com/favicon.ico' rel='icon'
type='image/x-icon'/>
 <link href='http://your-blog-URL-here.blogspot.com/' rel='canonical'/>
 <link href='https://plus.google.com/103914706589632755932' rel='Google+'/>
 <link href='https://plus.google.com/103914706589632755932' rel='publisher'/>
 <base href='http://your-blog-URL-here.blogspot.com'/>
 <meta content='INDEX, FOLLOW' name='ROBOTS'/>
 <meta content='blogging,seo tips,online business,google adsense'
name='keywords'/>
 <link href='https://plus.google.com/your-GooglePlus-URL' rel='author'/>
 <link href='http://your-blog-URL-here.blogspot.com/' rel='openid.delegate'/>
 <b:if cond='data:blog.isMobile'>
  <b:if cond='data:blog.url == data:blog.homepageUrl'>
   <title><data:blog.pageTitle/></title>
   <meta content=" name='description'/>
   <meta content='width=device-width,initial-scale=1.0,minimum-
scale=1.0,maximum-scale=1.0' name='viewport'/>
   <link expr:href='data:blog.url' rel='canonical'/>
   <b:else/>
   <title><data:blog.pageName/></title>
      <meta expr:content='data:blog.metaDescription' property='og:description'/>
   <link expr:href='data:blog.url' rel='canonical'/>
   <meta content='width=device-width,initial-scale=1.0,minimum-
scale=1.0,maximum-scale=1.0' name='viewport'/>
  </b:if>
  <b:else/>
  <b:if cond='data:blog.url == data:blog.homepageUrl'>
   <title><data:blog.pageTitle/></title>
   <meta content=" name='description'/>
```

```
<link expr:href='data:blog.url' rel='canonical'/>
<meta content='width=1100' name='viewport'/>
<b:else/>
<title>
  <data:blog.pageName/></title>
<meta expr:content='data:blog.metaDescription' property='og:description'/>
<link expr:href='data:blog.url' rel='canonical'/>
<meta content='width=1100' name='viewport'/>
</b:if>
</b:if>
<b:skin><![CDATA[
]]></b:skin>
<style type='text/css'>
  #navbar,#navbar-iframe {
    height:0;
    display:block;
    visibility:hidden;
  }
  body, html {
    margin:0 auto;
    padding:0;
    width:1005px;
    color:#2d2d2d;
    font-family:georgia;
  }
  img {
    border:1px groove #F1F1F1;
    box-shadow:0px 1px 2px 0px rgba(0,0,0,0.55);
    border-radius: 10px 10px 10px 10px;
    text-align:center;
  }
  h2 {
    text-transform:capitalize;
  }
  h4, h5, h6 {
    font-size:13px;
    font-family:georgia;
  }
  body {
    margin:0 auto;
    color:#2d2d2d;
    font-size:16px;
    text-align:center;
    border-radius:14px;
```

```css
  background-color:#ffffff;
  font:georgia;
}
li {
  font:georgia;
  font-size:13px;
}
h1 {
  background:none;
  font-size:27px;
  color:#1CB3EA;
  text-transform:uppercase;
  font-family: sans-serif;
  width:100%;
  font-weight:bold;
}
h1 a {
  color:#1CB3EA;
  background:none;
  text-transform:uppercase;
  font-family: sans-serif;
  width:100%;
  font-weight:bold;
}
img {
  text-align:center;
}
iframe {
  border:none;
  overflow:hidden;
}
a {
  color:#50b7dc;
  text-decoration:none;
  border:none;
  font-weight:normal;
}
a:hover {
  color:#DB3CB1;
  text-decoration:underline;
  border:none;
  font-weight:normal;
}
a img {
```

```
      border-width:0;
      border:none;
    }
#top-wrapper {
    width:100%;
    margin:0 auto;
    padding:0;
    text-align:center;
    font-family:georgia;
    border-bottom:none;
    line-height:1.200;
    margin:0px 0px 0px 0px;
    padding:10px 0px 0px 0px;
    background:#87BEEC;
    border-bottom:1px solid #2D2D2D;
    box-shadow:0px 1px 2px 0px rgba(0,0,0,0.55);
    border-radius: 10px 10px 10px 10px;
    }
.top2 h2 {
    display:block;
    }
.top2 .widget {
    padding:10px 0px 10px 0px;
    padding:0;
    margin:0 auto;
    background:#87BEEC;
    border:none;
    }
.top1 {
    margin-bottom:0px;
    background-color:#2D2D2D;
    border-bottom:1px solid #D4D0C8;
    width:100%;
    float:left;
    }
.top1 h2 {
    display:block;
    width:100%;
    float:left;
    }
#header-inner {
    margin:0 auto;
    padding-top:10px;
    width:100%;
```

```css
}
#header a {
  color:#263844;
  text-decoration:none;
}
#header {
  margin:0 auto;
  padding:0;
  width:100%;
  text-transform:none;
  letter-spacing:0.01em;
  line-height:1.3em;
  font-family:georgia;
  color:#FC9645;
  font-weight:normal;
  font-size:14px;
  margin-top:0px;
  box-shadow:0px 1px 2px 0px rgba(0,0,0,0.55);
  border-radius: 10px 10px 10px 10px;
}
.description {
  margin:0 auto;
  padding:0px;
  text-transform:none;
  letter-spacing:0.01em;
  line-height:2.0em;
  font:georgia;
  color:#EEEDEA;
  font-weight:normal;
  margin-top:-17px;
  font-size:16px;
  width:900px;
}
.description h2 {
  font-family:georgia;
  width:900px;
}
#header img {
  margin-left:auto;
}
#PageList1{
  padding:5px 0px 10px 0px;
  margin:10px 0px 0px 0px;
}
```

```css
#outer-wrapper {
  background:#ffffff;
  border:none;
  width:100%;
  margin:0 auto;
  padding:2px 0px 0px 0px;
  text-align:left;
  font-family:georgia;
}
#content-wrapper {
  float:left;
  width:710px;
  margin:0 auto;
  padding:0px;
  text-align:left;
  font-family:georgia;
}
#crosscol-wrapper {
  clear:both;
  width:auto;
  overflow-wrap:break-word;
  overflow:hidden;
  margin:0px;
  padding:0px 0px 0px 0px;
}
.crosscol {
  color:#242424;
  line-height:1.4em;
}
.crosscol .widget {
  padding:5px 5px;
  text-align:left;
  border-bottom:none;
  margin:0 0 5px;
}
#main-wrapper {
  padding:2px 0px 0px 10px;
  border:none;
  width:700px;
  margin:0 auto;
  float:left;
  overflow-wrap:break-word;
  overflow:hidden;
}
```

```css
#sidebar2-wrapper {
  margin:0px;
  padding:20px 0px 20px 10px;
  width : 240px;
  overflow-wrap:break-word;
  overflow:inherit;
  text-align:left;
  float:left;
}
#sidebar2-wrapper h2 {
  font-size:13px;
  margin:0;
  padding:10px 20px 7px 10px;
  letter-spacing:0.01em;
  line-height:1.4em;
  text-transform:capitalize;
  border:0px solid #2D2D2D;
  text-align:center;
  border:0px solid #000000;
  background:#2D2D2D;
  border-radius:14px;
  color:#ffffff;
  margin-bottom:10px;
}
h2 {
  margin:0 0 0.75em;
  font-family:georgia;
  line-height:1.4em;
  text-transform:capitalize;
  letter-spacing:0.01em;
  color:#2D2D2D;
  font-size:14px;
}
.post {
  margin:-5px 0px 0px 5px;
  border-bottom:1px solid #F1F1F1;
  padding:0px 10px 10px 10px;
  background:none;
  border-radius:14px;
  width:650px;
}
.post h1 {
  background:url(http://www.pcnet-online.web.id/_sdk/blogtina/h2-post-title.png)
no-repeat;
```

```css
   border-radius:14px;
   background:#1cb3ea;
   font-family:Arial;
   margin:0.25em 0 0;
   padding :0px 10px 0px 10px;
   font-size:14px;
   font-weight:normal;
   color:#1CB3EB;
   border:1px solid #D5D1CA;
   box-shadow:0px 1px 2px 0px rgba(0,0,0,0.55);
   text-transform:capitalize;
}
.post h1 a:link {
   font-weight:normal;
   border-radius: 14px;
   background: #1cb3ea;
   display:block;
   text-decoration:none;
   color:#1CB3EA;
   text-transform:capitalize;
}
.post h1 active {
   font-weight:normal;
   border-radius: 14px;
   background: #1cb3ea;
   display:block;
   text-decoration:none;
   text-transform:capitalize;
   color:#1CB3EA;
}
.post h1 visited {
   border-radius: 14px;
   background: #1cb3ea;
   color:#1CB3EA;
   text-decoration :none;
   text-transform:capitalize;
   font-weight:normal;
}
.post h1 a:hover {
   border-radius:14px;
   background:none;
   color:#64CA64;
   text-decoration:underline;
   text-transform:capitalize;
```

```css
   font-weight:normal;
 }
.post h4 {
  font-family:georgia;
  margin:0px;
  padding:5px 0px 0px 0px;
    font-size:11px;
  font-weight:normal;
  color:#2D2D2D;
}
.post-body {
  padding:0px 5px 5px 5px;
  margin:0 0 0.75em;
  line-height:1.6em;
}
.post-body blockquote {
  line-height:1.6em;
}
.post-footer {
  margin:0.75em 0;
  color:#242424;
  text-transform:none;
  letter-spacing:0.01em;
  font-family:georgia;
  line-height:1.4em;
  background-color:#1cb3ea;
  background:none;
}
.post img, table.tr-caption-container {
  padding-top:4px;
  border:none;
  background:none;
}
.tr-caption-container img {
  border:none;
  padding:0;
}
.post blockquote {
  background:#F1F1F1;
  border:1px solid #BDBEB2;
  box-shadow:0px 1px 2px 0px rgba(0,0,0,0.55);
  margin:0px;
  padding:20px 5px 20px 10px;
  font-size:13px;
```

```
    font-family:georgia;
    width:470px;
    height:auto;
    overflow:auto;
    line-height:1.300;
    border-left: 7px solid #FB9442;
  }
  .sidebar2 .PopularPosts h5 {
    background:#FB9341;
    margin:0;
    padding:10px 20px;
    border:none;
    font-family:georgia;
    line-height:1.4em;
    text-transform:uppercase;
    letter-spacing:0.01em;
    color:#ffffff;
    border-radius: 15px;
    text-align:center;
    text-decoration:none;
  }
  .sidebar2 .PopularPosts {
    margin:0;
    padding:0;
  }
  .sidebar2 .PopularPosts .widget-content {
    padding:0;
    background:#ffffff;
  }
  .widget-content {
    background-color:#ffffff;
    padding:0px 0px 0px 0px;
    font:georgia;
    font-size:13px;
  }
  .sidebar2 .PopularPosts {
    text-transform:none;
    padding:0;
    font:georgia;
    font-size:13px;
  }
  .sidebar2 .PopularPosts ul {
    margin:0;
    padding:0;
```

```css
  font:georgia;
  font-size:13px;
  text-decoration:none;
}
.sidebar2 .PopularPosts ul li {
  margin:0;
  padding:15px 20px;
  text-indent:0;
  line-height:1.3em;
  list-style:none;
  display:block;
  border-top:none;
  font:georgia;
  font-size:13px;
  color:#1CB3EA;
}
.sidebar2 .PopularPosts .item-content {
  margin:0;
  padding:0;
}
.sidebar2 .PopularPosts .item-title {
  font-size:13px;
  font-weight:bold;
  text-decoration:none;
  text-transform:uppercase;
  font:georgia;
  font-size:14px;
}
.sidebar2 .PopularPosts .item-title a {
  text-decoration:none;
  color:#FB9341;
  font:georgia;
  font-size:14px;
}
.sidebar2 .PopularPosts .item-title a:hover {
  color:#1CB3EA;
}
.sidebar2 .PopularPosts .item-snippet {
  font-size:12px;
  padding:0;
  margin:2px 0 0;
  line-height:1.4em;
  color:#242424;
}
```

```css
.sidebar2 .PopularPosts img {
  background:#ffffff;
  border:none;
  padding:4px;
}
.sidebar2 .label-size {
  background:#f1f1f1;
  margin:0 3px 5px 0;
  padding:6px;
  text-transform:uppercase;
  border:none;
  float:left;
  font-family:arial;
  text-decoration:none;
  font-size:7px;
  color:#333;
  position:relative;
}
.label-size:hover {
  background:#f0f0f0;
  border:none;
  text-decoration:none;
  color:#2288bb;
}
.sidebar2 .label-size a {
  color:#666;
  text-transform:uppercase;
  text-decoration:none;
}
.profile-img {
  float:left;
  border:none;
  border:0px;
  margin-right:8px;
}
.g-follow {
  background-repeat:no-repeat;
}
.profile-data {
  margin:0px;
  text-transform:uppercase;
  letter-spacing:0.01em;
  font-family:georgia;
  color:#242424;
```

```css
    font-weight:bold;
    line-height:1.5em;
  }
  .profile-datablock {
    margin:0.5em 0 0.5em;
  }
  .profile-textblock {
    margin:0.5em 0;
    line-height:1.5em;
  }
  .profile-link {
    font-family:georgia;
    text-transform:Capitalize;
    letter-spacing:0.01em;
    background-repeat:no-repeat;
  }
  #footer {
    width:962px;
    clear:both;
    margin:0 auto;
    padding:0;
    line-height:1.5em;
    text-transform:none;
    letter-spacing:0.01em;
    text-align :center;
    background:none;
  }
  .footer .widget {
    margin:0;
    padding:15px 0;
    border-top:none;
    background:none;
  }
  #credit-wrapper {
    background:none;
    width:962px;
    margin:0 auto;
    border:none;
    border-width:0 1px;
    clear:both;
  }
  #credit-wrapper a {
    color:#FC9443;
  }
```

```css
#link-wrapper {
  width:962px;
  line-height:1.6em;
  text-align:center;
  font-family: georgia;
  font-size:12px;
  color:#666;
  padding:20px 0;
}
.post-footer {
  display:none;
}
#TemplateSEOBlogspot {
  text-align:center;
  text-decoration:none;
  font-size:12px;
  font:georgia;
  color:#2D2D2D;
  overflow:hidden;
}
#TemplateSEOBlogspot a {
  text-decoration:none;
}
#TemplateSEOBlogspot img {
  width:128px;
  height:183px;
  border:0px;
  text-shadow:none;
}
.highlight-point{
  text-align:left;
  font-family:georgia;
  font-size:12px;
  text-decoration:none;
  background-color:#F1F1F1;
  margin:0px;
  padding:7px 10px 7px 12px;
  color: #666666;
  font-weight:normal;
}
.img-author img {
  float:left;
  text-align:left;
  margin:0px;
```

```css
  padding:7px 6px 7px 0px;
  width:42px;
  height:50px;
}
/*-- start:menu-your-blog-URL-here --*/
.iwd-img {
  text-align:center;
}
.menu-tina h2 {
  font-weight:bold;
  font-size:12px;
  text-align:center;
  font-family:sans-serif;
  text-transform:none;
  color:#4F474F;
  background:none;
  background:#1CB3EA;
  margin-bottom:6px;
  padding:4px 0px 4px 0px;
  border-top:1px inset #ffffff;
  border-bottom:1px groove #D4D0C8;
  box-shadow:0px 1px 2px 0px rgba(0,0,0,0.55);
}
.menu-tina h2 a {
  text-decoration:none;
  color:#ffffff;
  text-transform:uppercase;
  background:none;
  background:#1CB3EA;
  background:none;
}
.menu-tina h2 a:hover {
  text-decoration:none;
  color:#EC1A23;
  text-transform:uppercase;
  background:none;
  background:#1CB3EA;
}
/*-- end:menu-your-blog-URL-here --*/
#ticker {
  height:24px;
  overflow:hidden;
  border:1px inset #ffffff;
  box-shadow:0px 1px 2px 0px rgba(0,0,0,0.55);
```

```css
  font-weight:normal;
  border-top:1px outset #FB9442;
}
#ticker li {
  margin-top:-11px;
  height:32px;
  font-weight:bold;
  font-size:14px;
}
#ticker li a:link, #ticker li a:visited, #ticker li a:active {
  color:#2d2d2d;
}
#ticker li a:hover {
  color:#ffffff;
}
.bar {
  background-color:#111;
  color:#f0f0f0;
  box-shadow:0px 0px 2px #333;
  line-height:25;
  padding:0px 20px;
}
.bar a {
  color:#DDD;
  text-decoration:none;
}
.bar a:hover {
  color:#FFFFFF;
}
.headme-bottom-browser {
  margin:0 auto;
  font-size:15px;
  color:#ffffff;
  display:block;
  z-index:999;
  text-align:center;
  position:fixed;
  /*top:-20px;*/
  top:0px;
  left:0px;
  width:100%;
  background-color:#64CA64;
  border-bottom:1px groove #ffffff;
  border-radius:0px;
```

```css
  }
  .headme-bottom-browser{
    color:#fafafa;
    font-weight:bold;
  }
  .flattr-me {
    text-align:left;
    /*float:left;*/
  }
  .kekiri {
    text-align:left;
  }
  .kekiri img {
    text-align:left;
    margin:2px 12px 2px 0px;
    float:left;
  }
  hr {
    border:1px solid #EDEDED;
  }
  .adsense-seo {
    float:right;
    padding:0px 2px 2px 12px;
    border:0px;
    text-align:left;
    margin:1px;
    text-decoration:none;
    background:none;
    color:#1CB3EA;
    text-transform:none;
    text-decoration:none;
  }
  .linknofo {
    text-align:center;
    font-size:14px;
    font-weight:normal;
    text-decoration:none;
  }
  #subs, #subz {
    border:1px solid #E2E2E2;
  }
</style>
&lt;/head&gt;&lt;!--
<head/>
```

```
--&gt;
<body>
  <div itemscope=" itemtype='http://schema.org/Blog'>
    <script src='https://ajax.googleapis.com/ajax/libs/jquery/1.6.4/jquery.min.js'/>
    <script type='text/javascript'>
    function tick(){$(&#39;#ticker li:first&#39;).slideUp( function () {
$(this).appendTo($(&#39;#ticker&#39;)).slideDown(); });}setInterval(function(){ tick
() }, 5000);
    </script>
    <b:section class='navbar' id='navbar' maxwidgets='1' showaddelement='no'/>
    <div id='top-wrapper'>
      <div class='headme-bottom-browser' id='ticker'>
        <ul>
          <b:if cond='data:blog.pageName != &quot;item&quot;'>
            <li>
              How to Optimize your Blogspot and Increase Blog Visibility in Search Engine
            </li>
            <li>
              This Blog is Dedicated to All Indonesian Bloggers - your-blog-URL-
here.blogspot.com - 2014
            </li>
            <li>
              Telah hadir Kursus Online Murah Desain dan Pemrograman Website
            </li>
            <li>
              Belajar Desain Website dari NOL
            </li>
            <li>
              Silahkan Daftarkan diri Anda:
              <span itemprop='url'>
                <a href='http://www.pcnet-online.web.id' target='_blank' title='Kursus
Desain Website Murah - Kelas Online - Online Classes - Indonesian Web Developer
Academy'>
                  www.pcnet-online.web.id
                </a>
              </span>
            </li>
          </b:if>
        </ul>
      </div>
      <b:section class='top1' id='top1' preferred='yes'>
        <b:widget id='Navbar1' locked='false' title='Navbar' type='Navbar'>
          <b:includable id='main'>&lt;script type=&quot;text/javascript&quot;&gt;
    function setAttributeOnload(object, attribute, val) {
```

```
    if(window.addEventListener) {
      window.addEventListener(&#39;load&#39;,
        function(){ object[attribute] = val; }, false);
    } else {
      window.attachEvent(&#39;onload&#39;, function(){ object[attribute] = val; });
    }
  }
&lt;/script&gt;
&lt;div id=&quot;navbar-iframe-container&quot;&gt;&lt;/div&gt;
&lt;script type=&quot;text/javascript&quot;
src=&quot;https://apis.google.com/js/plusone.js&quot;&gt;&lt;/script&gt;
&lt;script type=&quot;text/javascript&quot;&gt;
      gapi.load(&quot;gapi.iframes:gapi.iframes.style.bubble&quot;, function() {
        if (gapi.iframes &amp;&amp; gapi.iframes.getContext) {
          gapi.iframes.getContext().openChild({
              url:
&#39;https://www.blogger.com/navbar.g?targetBlogID\075677716052896247011\46bl
ogName\75Blogging+With+Tina-
Andrew\46publishMode\75PUBLISH_MODE_BLOGSPOT\46navbarType\75LIGHT\46layo
utType\75LAYOUTS\46searchRoot\75http://go-windows-
net.blogspot.com/search\46blogLocale\75en\46v\0752\46homepageUrl\75http://go-
windows-
net.blogspot.com/\46blogFollowUrl\75https://plus.google.com/10391470658963275593
2\46vt\75-16947386076670880614&#39;,
              where: document.getElementById(&quot;navbar-iframe-container&quot;),
              id: &quot;navbar-iframe&quot;
          });
        }
      });
    &lt;/script&gt;&lt;script type=&quot;text/javascript&quot;&gt;
(function() {
var script = document.createElement(&#39;script&#39;);
script.type = &#39;text/javascript&#39;;
script.src =
&#39;//pagead2.googlesyndication.com/pagead/js/google_top_exp.js&#39;;
var head = document.getElementsByTagName(&#39;head&#39;)[0];
if (head) {
head.appendChild(script);
}})();
&lt;/script&gt;
</b:includable>
        </b:widget>
        <b:widget id='Header1' locked='false' title='Blogging With Tina-Andrew
(Header)' type='Header'>
```

```
<b:includable id='main'>
  <b:if cond='data:useImage'>
    <b:if cond='data:imagePlacement == &quot;BEHIND&quot;'>
      <!--
```
Show image as background to text. You can't really calculate the width reliably in JS because margins are not taken into account by any of clientWidth, offsetWidth or scrollWidth, so we don't force a minimum width if the user is using shrink to fit.
This results in a margin-width's worth of pixels being cropped. If the user is not using shrink to fit then we expand the header.
```
      -->
          <b:if cond='data:mobile'>
            <div id='header-inner'>
              <div class='titlewrapper' style='background: transparent'>
                <h1 class='title' style='background: transparent; border-width: 0px'>
                  <b:include name='title'/>
                </h1>
              </div>
              <b:include name='description'/>
            </div>
            <b:else/>
            <div expr:style='&quot;background-image: url(\&quot;&quot; +
data:sourceUrl + &quot;\&quot;); &quot;            + &quot;background-
position: &quot;            + data:backgroundPositionStyleStr + &quot;; &quot;
+ data:widthStyleStr            + &quot;min-height: &quot; + data:height
+ &quot;_height: &quot; + data:height            + &quot;background-repeat:
no-repeat; &quot;' id='header-inner'>
              <div class='titlewrapper' style='background: transparent'>
                <h1 class='title' style='background: transparent; border-width: 0px'>
                  <b:include name='title'/>
                </h1>
              </div>
              <b:include name='description'/>
            </div>
          </b:if>
          <b:else/>
          <!--Show the image only-->
          <div id='header-inner'>
            <a expr:href='data:blog.homepageUrl' style='display: block'>
              <img expr:alt='data:title' expr:height='data:height'
expr:id='data:widget.instanceId + &quot;_headerimg&quot;' expr:src='data:sourceUrl'
expr:width='data:width' style='display: block'/>
            </a>
            <!--Show the description-->
```

```
          <b:if cond='data:imagePlacement ==
&quot;BEFORE_DESCRIPTION&quot;'>
              <b:include name='description'/>
            </b:if>
          </div>
        </b:if>
        <b:else/>
        <!--No header image -->
        <div id='header-inner'>
          <div class='titlewrapper'>
            <h1 class='title'>
              <b:include name='title'/>
            </h1>
          </div>
          <b:include name='description'/>
        </div>
      </b:if>
    </b:includable>
    <b:includable id='description'>
      <div class='descriptionwrapper'>
        <p class='description'>
          <span>
            <data:description/>
          </span>
        </p>
      </div>
    </b:includable>
    <b:includable id='title'>
      <b:if cond='data:blog.url == data:blog.homepageUrl'>
        <data:title/>
        <b:else/>
        <a expr:href='data:blog.homepageUrl'>
          <data:title/>
        </a>
      </b:if>
    </b:includable>
  </b:widget>
  <b:widget id='HTML4' locked='false' title='' type='HTML'>
    <b:includable id='main'>
      <!-- only display title if it's non-empty -->
      <b:if cond='data:title != &quot;&quot;'>
        <h2 class='title'>
          <data:title/>
        </h2>
```

```
      </b:if>
      <div class='widget-content'>
        <data:content/>
      </div>
    </b:includable>
  </b:widget>
  <b:widget id='HTML2' locked='false' title='' type='HTML'>
    <b:includable id='main'>
        <!-- only display title if it's non-empty -->
        <b:if cond='data:title != &quot;&quot;'>
          <h2 class='title'>
            <data:title/>
          </h2>
        </b:if>
        <div class='widget-content'>
          <data:content/>
        </div>
      </b:includable>
  </b:widget>
  </b:section>
</div>
<!-- article close -->
<div id='outer-wrapper'>
  <div id='wrap2'>
    <div id='content-wrapper'>
      <div id='main-wrapper'>
        <div id='crosscol-wrapper' style='text-align:center'>
          <b:section class='crosscol' id='crosscol'/>
        </div>
        <b:section class='main' id='main' showaddelement='no'>
          <b:widget id='Blog1' locked='true' title='Blog Posts' type='Blog'>
            <b:includable id='main' var='top'>
              <b:if cond='data:mobile == &quot;false&quot;'>
                <!-- posts -->
                <div itemprop='headline'>
                  <b:include data='top' name='status-message'/>
                  <data:defaultAdStart/>
                  <b:loop values='data:posts' var='post'>
                    <b:if cond='data:post.isDateStart'>
                      <b:if cond='data:post.isFirstPost == &quot;false&quot;'>
                        &lt;/div&gt;&lt;/div&gt;
                      </b:if>
                    </b:if>
                    <b:if cond='data:post.isDateStart'>
```

```
&lt;div class=&quot;date-outer&quot;&gt;
</b:if>
<b:if cond='data:post.dateHeader'>
  <h4 class='date-header'>
    <span>
      <data:post.dateHeader/>
    </span>
    <span class='post-author vcard'>
      <b:if cond='data:top.showAuthor'>
        <b:if cond='data:post.authorProfileUrl'>
          <span class='fn' itemprop='Author'>
            <meta expr:content='data:post.authorProfileUrl'
itemprop='url'/>

            <a expr:href='data:post.authorProfileUrl' rel='author'>
              <span itemprop='name'>
                <data:post.author/>
              </span>
            </a>
          </span>
        </b:if>
      </b:if>
    </span>
  </h4>
</b:if>
<b:if cond='data:post.isDateStart'>
  &lt;div class=&quot;date-posts&quot;&gt;
</b:if>
<div class='post-outer'>
  <b:include data='post' name='post'/>
  <b:if cond='data:blog.pageType == &quot;static_page&quot;'>
    <b:include data='post' name='comment_picker'/>
  </b:if>
  <b:if cond='data:blog.pageType == &quot;item&quot;'>
    <b:include data='post' name='comment_picker'/>
  </b:if>
</div>
<b:if cond='data:post.includeAd'>
  <b:if cond='data:post.isFirstPost'>
    <data:defaultAdEnd/>
    <b:else/>
    <data:adEnd/>
  </b:if>
  <div class='inline-ad'>
    <data:adCode/>
```

```
            </div>
            <data:adStart/>
          </b:if>
        </b:loop>
        <b:if cond='data:numPosts != 0'>
          &lt;/div&gt;&lt;/div&gt;
        </b:if>
        <data:adEnd/>
      </div>
      <!-- navigation -->
      <b:include name='nextprev'/>
      <!-- feed links -->
      <b:include name='feedLinks'/>
      <b:if cond='data:top.showStars'>
        <script src='//www.google.com/jsapi' type='text/javascript'/>
        <script type='text/javascript'>
          google.load(&quot;annotations&quot;, &quot;1&quot;,
{&quot;locale&quot;: &quot;<data:top.languageCode/>&quot;});
          function initialize() {
            google.annotations.setApplicationId(<data:top.blogspotReviews/>);
            google.annotations.createAll();
            google.annotations.fetch();
          }
          google.setOnLoadCallback(initialize);
        </script>
      </b:if>
      <b:else/>
      <b:include name='mobile-main'/>
    </b:if>
    <b:if cond='data:top.showDummy'>
      <data:top.dummyBootstrap/>
    </b:if>
  </b:includable>
  <b:includable id='backlinkDeleteIcon' var='backlink'>
    <span expr:class='&quot;item-control &quot; +
data:backlink.adminClass'>
      </span>
  </b:includable>
  <b:includable id='backlinks' var='post'>
    <a name='links'/>
    <h6>
      <data:post.backlinksLabel/>
    </h6>
    <b:if cond='data:post.numBacklinks != 0'>
```

```
<dl class='comments-block' id='comments-block'>
  <b:loop values='data:post.backlinks' var='backlink'>
    <div class='collapsed-backlink backlink-control'>
      <dt class='comment-title'>
        <span class='backlink-toggle-zippy'>
          
        </span>
        <a expr:href='data:backlink.url' rel='nofollow'>
          <data:backlink.title/>
        </a>
        <b:include data='backlink' name='backlinkDeleteIcon'/>
      </dt>
      <dd class='comment-body collapseable'>
        <data:backlink.snippet/>
      </dd>
      <dd class='comment-footer collapseable'>
        <span class='comment-author'>
          <data:post.authorLabel/>
          <data:backlink.author/>
        </span>
        <span class='comment-timestamp'>
          <data:post.timestampLabel/>
          <data:backlink.timestamp/>
        </span>
      </dd>
    </div>
  </b:loop>
</dl>
</b:if>
<p class='comment-footer'>
  <a class='comment-link' expr:href='data:post.createLinkUrl'
expr:id='data:widget.instanceId + &quot;_backlinks-create-link&quot;' target='_blank'>
    <data:post.createLinkLabel/>
  </a>
</p>
</b:includable>
<b:includable id='comment-form' var='post'>
  <div class='comment-form'>
    <a name='comment-form'/>
    <b:if cond='data:mobile'>
      <h4 id='comment-post-message'>
        <a expr:id='data:widget.instanceId + &quot;_comment-editor-
toggle-link&quot;' href='javascript:void(0)'>
          <data:postCommentMsg/>
```

```
          </a>
          </h4>
          <p>
            <data:blogCommentMessage/>
          </p>
          <data:blogTeamBlogMessage/>
          <a expr:href='data:post.commentFormIframeSrc' id='comment-editor-
src'/>
          <iframe allowtransparency='true' class='blogger-iframe-colorize
blogger-comment-from-post' frameborder='0' height='310' id='comment-editor'
name='comment-editor' src=" style='display: none' width='370'/>
          <b:else/>
          <h4 id='comment-post-message'>
            <data:postCommentMsg/>
          </h4>
          <p>
            <data:blogCommentMessage/>
          </p>
          <data:blogTeamBlogMessage/>
          <a expr:href='data:post.commentFormIframeSrc' id='comment-editor-
src'/>
          <iframe allowtransparency='true' class='blogger-iframe-colorize
blogger-comment-from-post' frameborder='0' height='310' id='comment-editor'
name='comment-editor' src=" width='370'/>
          </b:if>
          <data:post.friendConnectJs/>
          <data:post.cmtfpIframe/>
          <script type='text/javascript'>
            BLOG_CMT_createIframe(&#39;<data:post.appRpcRelayPath/>&#39;,
&#39;<data:post.communityId/>&#39;);
          </script>
        </div>
      </b:includable>
      <b:includable id='commentDeleteIcon' var='comment'>
        <span expr:class='&quot;item-control &quot; +
data:comment.adminClass'>
          <b:if cond='data:showCmtPopup'>
            <div class='goog-toggle-button'>
              <div class='goog-inline-block comment-action-icon'/>
            </div>
          </b:if>
        </span>
      </b:includable>
      <b:includable id='comment_count_picker' var='post'>
```

```
<b:if cond='data:post.commentSource == 1'>
  <span class='cmt_count_iframe_holder' expr:data-count='data:post.numComments' expr:data-onclick='data:post.addCommentOnclick' expr:data-post-url='data:post.url' expr:data-url='data:post.canonicalUrl'>
  </span>
  <b:else/>
  <a class='comment-link' expr:href='data:post.addCommentUrl' expr:onclick='data:post.addCommentOnclick'>
    <data:post.commentLabelFull/>
    :
  </a>
</b:if>
</b:includable>
<b:includable id='comment_picker' var='post'>
  <b:if cond='data:post.commentSource == 1'>
    <b:include data='post' name='iframe_comments'/>
    <b:else/>
    <b:if cond='data:post.showThreadedComments'>
      <b:include data='post' name='threaded_comments'/>
      <b:else/>
      <b:include data='post' name='comments'/>
    </b:if>
  </b:if>
</b:includable>
<b:includable id='comments' var='post'>
  <div class='comments' id='comments'>
    <a name='comments'/>
    <b:if cond='data:post.allowComments'>
      <h6>
        <data:post.commentLabelFull/>
        :
      </h6>
      <b:if cond='data:post.commentPagingRequired'>
        <span class='paging-control-container'>
          <b:if cond='data:post.hasOlderLinks'>
            <a expr:class='data:post.oldLinkClass' expr:href='data:post.oldestLinkUrl'>
              <data:post.oldestLinkText/>
            </a>
             
            <a expr:class='data:post.oldLinkClass' expr:href='data:post.olderLinkUrl'>
              <data:post.olderLinkText/>
            </a>
```

```
                 
            </b:if>
            <data:post.commentRangeText/>
            <b:if cond='data:post.hasNewerLinks'>
             
            <a expr:class='data:post.newLinkClass'
expr:href='data:post.newerLinkUrl'>
                <data:post.newerLinkText/>
            </a>
             
            <a expr:class='data:post.newLinkClass'
expr:href='data:post.newestLinkUrl'>
                <data:post.newestLinkText/>
            </a>
            </b:if>
            </span>
            </b:if>
            <div expr:id='data:widget.instanceId + &quot;_comments-block-
wrapper&quot;'>
                <dl expr:class='data:post.avatarIndentClass' id='comments-block'>
                <b:loop values='data:post.comments' var='comment'>
                <dt expr:class='&quot;comment-author &quot; +
data:comment.authorClass' expr:id='data:comment.anchorName'>
                    <b:if cond='data:comment.favicon'>
                    <img expr:src='data:comment.favicon' height='16px'
style='margin-bottom:-2px;' width='16px'/>
                    </b:if>
                    <a expr:name='data:comment.anchorName'/>
                    <b:if cond='data:blog.enabledCommentProfileImages'>
                    <data:comment.authorAvatarImage/>
                    </b:if>
                    <b:if cond='data:comment.authorUrl'>
                    <a expr:href='data:comment.authorUrl'>
                        <data:comment.author/>
                    </a>
                    <b:else/>
                    <data:comment.author/>
                    </b:if>
                    <data:commentPostedByMsg/>
                </dt>
                <dd class='comment-body' expr:id='data:widget.instanceId +
data:comment.cmtBodyIdPostfix'>
                    <b:if cond='data:comment.isDeleted'>
                    <span class='deleted-comment'>
```

```
              <data:comment.body/>
            </span>
            <b:else/>
            <p>
              <data:comment.body/>
            </p>
          </b:if>
        </dd>
        <dd class='comment-footer'>
          <span class='comment-timestamp'>
            <a expr:href='data:comment.url' title='comment permalink'>
              <data:comment.timestamp/>
            </a>
            <b:include data='comment' name='commentDeleteIcon'/>
          </span>
        </dd>
      </b:loop>
    </dl>
  </div>
  <b:if cond='data:post.commentPagingRequired'>
    <span class='paging-control-container'>
      <a expr:class='data:post.oldLinkClass'
expr:href='data:post.oldestLinkUrl'>
          <data:post.oldestLinkText/>
      </a>
      <a expr:class='data:post.oldLinkClass'
expr:href='data:post.olderLinkUrl'>
          <data:post.olderLinkText/>
      </a>
       
      <data:post.commentRangeText/>
       
      <a expr:class='data:post.newLinkClass'
expr:href='data:post.newerLinkUrl'>
          <data:post.newerLinkText/>
      </a>
      <a expr:class='data:post.newLinkClass'
expr:href='data:post.newestLinkUrl'>
          <data:post.newestLinkText/>
      </a>
    </span>
  </b:if>
  <p class='comment-footer'>
    <b:if cond='data:post.embedCommentForm'>
```

```
<b:if cond='data:post.allowNewComments'>
  <b:include data='post' name='comment-form'/>
  <b:else/>
  <data:post.noNewCommentsText/>
</b:if>
<b:else/>
<b:if cond='data:post.allowComments'>
  <a expr:href='data:post.addCommentUrl'
expr:onclick='data:post.addCommentOnclick'>
      <data:postCommentMsg/>
  </a>
</b:if>
</b:if>
</p>
</b:if>
<b:if cond='data:showCmtPopup'>
  <div id='comment-popup'>
  <iframe allowtransparency='true' frameborder='0' id='comment-
actions' name='comment-actions' scrolling='no'>
      </iframe>
  </div>
</b:if>
<div id='backlinks-container'>
  <div expr:id='data:widget.instanceId + &quot;_backlinks-
container&quot;'>
      <b:if cond='data:post.showBacklinks'>
        <b:include data='post' name='backlinks'/>
      </b:if>
  </div>
</div>
</div>
</b:includable>
<b:includable id='feedLinks'>
  <b:if cond='data:blog.pageType != &quot;item&quot;'>
  <!-- Blog feed links -->
  <b:if cond='data:feedLinks'>
    <div class='blog-feeds'>
      <b:include data='feedLinks' name='feedLinksBody'/>
    </div>
  </b:if>
  <b:else/>
  <!--Post feed links -->
  <div class='post-feeds'>
    <b:loop values='data:posts' var='post'>
```

```
<b:if cond='data:post.allowComments'>
  <b:if cond='data:post.feedLinks'>
    <b:include data='post.feedLinks' name='feedLinksBody'/>
  </b:if>
</b:if>
</b:loop>
</div>
</b:if>
</b:includable>
<b:includable id='feedLinksBody' var='links'>
  <div class='feed-links'>
    <data:feedLinksMsg/>
    <b:loop values='data:links' var='f'>
      <a class='feed-link' expr:href='data:f.url' expr:type='data:f.mimeType'
target='_blank'>
        <data:f.name/>
        (
        <data:f.feedType/>
        )
      </a>
    </b:loop>
  </div>
</b:includable>
<b:includable id='iframe_comments' var='post'>
  <b:if cond='data:post.allowIframeComments'>
    <script expr:src='data:post.iframeCommentSrc' type='text/javascript'/>
    <div class='cmt_iframe_holder' expr:data-href='data:post.canonicalUrl'
expr:data-viewtype='data:post.viewType'/>
    <b:if cond='data:post.embedCommentForm == &quot;false&quot;'>
      <a expr:href='data:post.addCommentUrl'
expr:onclick='data:post.addCommentOnclick'>
        <data:postCommentMsg/>
      </a>
    </b:if>
  </b:if>
</b:includable>
<b:includable id='mobile-index-post' var='post'>
  <div class='mobile-date-outer date-outer'>
    <b:if cond='data:post.dateHeader'>
      <div class='date-header'>
        <span>
          <data:post.dateHeader/>
        </span>
      </div>
```

```
    </b:if>
    <div class='mobile-post-outer'>
      <a expr:href='data:post.url'>
        <h1 class='mobile-index-title entry-title' itemprop='name'>
          <data:post.title/>
        </h1>
        <div class='mobile-index-arrow'>
         &amp;rsaquo;
        </div>
        <div class='mobile-index-contents'>
          <b:if cond='data:post.thumbnailUrl'>
            <div class='mobile-index-thumbnail'>
              <div class='Image'>
                <img expr:src='data:post.thumbnailUrl'/>
              </div>
            </div>
          </b:if>
          <div class='post-body'>
            <b:if cond='data:post.snippet'>
              <data:post.snippet/>
            </b:if>
          </div>
        </div>
        <div style='clear: both;'/>
      </a>
      <div class='mobile-index-comment'>
        <b:if cond='data:blog.pageType != &quot;static_page&quot;'>
          <b:if cond='data:post.allowComments'>
            <b:if cond='data:post.numComments != 0'>
              <b:include data='post' name='comment_count_picker'/>
            </b:if>
          </b:if>
        </b:if>
      </div>
    </div>
  </div>
</b:includable>
<b:includable id='mobile-main' var='top'>
  <!-- posts -->
  <div itemprop='blogPost'>
    <b:include data='top' name='status-message'/>
    <b:if cond='data:blog.pageType == &quot;index&quot;'>
      <b:loop values='data:posts' var='post'>
        <b:include data='post' name='mobile-index-post'/>
```

```
        </b:loop>
        <b:else/>
        <b:loop values='data:posts' var='post'>
          <b:include data='post' name='mobile-post'/>
        </b:loop>
      </b:if>
    </div>
    <b:include name='mobile-nextprev'/>
  </b:includable>
  <b:includable id='mobile-nextprev'>
    <div class='blog-pager' id='blog-pager'>
      <b:if cond='data:newerPageUrl'>
        <div class='mobile-link-button' id='blog-pager-newer-link'>
        <a class='blog-pager-newer-link' expr:href='data:newerPageUrl'
expr:id='data:widget.instanceId + &quot;_blog-pager-newer-link&quot;'
expr:title='data:newerPageTitle'>
          &amp;lsaquo;
        </a>
      </div>
    </b:if>
      <b:if cond='data:olderPageUrl'>
        <div class='mobile-link-button' id='blog-pager-older-link'>
        <a class='blog-pager-older-link' expr:href='data:olderPageUrl'
expr:id='data:widget.instanceId + &quot;_blog-pager-older-link&quot;'
expr:title='data:olderPageTitle'>
          &amp;rsaquo;
        </a>
      </div>
    </b:if>
      <div class='mobile-link-button' id='blog-pager-home-link'>
        <a class='home-link' expr:href='data:blog.homepageUrl'>
          <data:homeMsg/>
        </a>
      </div>
      <div class='mobile-desktop-link'>
        <a class='home-link' expr:href='data:desktopLinkUrl'>
          <data:desktopLinkMsg/>
        </a>
      </div>
    </div>
    <div class='clear'/>
  </b:includable>
  <b:includable id='mobile-post' var='post'>
    <div class='date-outer'>
```

```
<b:if cond='data:post.dateHeader'>
  <h4 class='date-header'>
    <span>
      <data:post.dateHeader/>
    </span>
  </h4>
</b:if>
<div class='date-posts'>
  <div class='post-outer'>
    <div itemscope=" itemtype='http://schema.org/blogPost'>
      <b:if cond='data:post.thumbnailUrl'>
        <meta expr:content='data:post.thumbnailUrl' itemprop='url'/>
      </b:if>
      <b:if cond='data:post.title'>
        <h1 class='post-title entry-title' itemprop='name'>
          <b:if cond='data:post.link'>
            <a expr:href='data:post.link'>
              <data:post.title/>
            </a>
            <b:else/>
            <b:if cond='data:post.url'>
              <b:if cond='data:blog.url != data:post.url'>
                <a expr:href='data:post.url'>
                  <data:post.title/>
                </a>
                <b:else/>
                <data:post.title/>
              </b:if>
              <b:else/>
              <data:post.title/>
            </b:if>
          </b:if>
        </h1>
      </b:if>
      <div class='post-header'>
        <div class='post-header-line-1'/>
      </div>
      <div class='post-body entry-content' expr:id='&quot;post-body-
&quot; + data:post.id' itemprop='blogPost'>
        <data:post.body/>
        <div style='clear: both;'/>
        <!-- clear for photos floats -->
      </div>
      <div class='post-footer'>
```

```
<div class='post-footer-line post-footer-line-1'>
  <span class='post-author vcard'>
    <b:if cond='data:top.showAuthor'>
      <b:if cond='data:post.authorProfileUrl'>
        <span class='fn' itemprop='author'>
          <meta expr:content='data:post.authorProfileUrl' itemprop='url'/>
          <a expr:href='data:post.authorProfileUrl' rel='author' title='author profile'>
            <span itemprop='name'>
              <data:post.author/>
            </span>
          </a>
        </span>
        <b:else/>
        <span class='fn' itemprop='Author'>
          <br/>
          <meta expr:content='data:post.authorProfileUrl' itemprop='url'/>
          <abbr title='Author of your-blog-URL-here.blogspot.com'>
            <a expr:href='data:post.authorProfileUrl' rel='author' title='Author Profile of your-blog-URL-here.blogspot.com on Google+'>
              <span itemprop='name'>
                <data:post.author/>
              </span>
            </a>
          </abbr>
        </span>
      </b:if>
    </b:if>
  </span>
  <span class='post-timestamp'>
    <b:if cond='data:top.showTimestamp'>
      <data:top.timestampLabel/>
      <b:if cond='data:post.url'>
        <meta expr:content='data:post.canonicalUrl' itemprop='url'/>
        <a class='timestamp-link' expr:href='data:post.url' rel='bookmark' title='permanent link'>
          <abbr class='published' expr:title='data:post.timestampISO8601' itemprop='datePublished'>
            <data:post.timestamp/>
          </abbr>
        </a>
```

```
          </b:if>
        </b:if>
      </span>
      <span class='post-comment-link'>
        <b:if cond='data:blog.pageType != &quot;item&quot;'>
          <b:if cond='data:blog.pageType !=
&quot;static_page&quot;'>
            <b:if cond='data:post.allowComments'>
              <b:include data='post' name='comment_count_picker'/>
            </b:if>
          </b:if>
        </b:if>
      </span>
    </div>
    <div class='post-footer-line post-footer-line-2'>
      <b:if cond='data:top.showMobileShare'>
        <div class='mobile-link-button goog-inline-block' id='mobile-
share-button'>
          <a href='javascript:void(0);'>
            <data:shareMsg/>
          </a>
        </div>
      </b:if>
    </div>
  </div>
</div>
<b:if cond='data:blog.pageType == &quot;static_page&quot;'>
  <b:include data='post' name='comment_picker'/>
</b:if>
<b:if cond='data:blog.pageType == &quot;item&quot;'>
  <b:include data='post' name='comment_picker'/>
</b:if>
    </div>
  </div>
</div>
</b:includable>
<b:includable id='nextprev'>
  <div class='blog-pager' id='blog-pager'>
    <b:if cond='data:newerPageUrl'>
      <span id='blog-pager-newer-link'>
        <a class='blog-pager-newer-link' expr:href='data:newerPageUrl'
expr:id='data:widget.instanceId + &quot;_blog-pager-newer-link&quot;'
expr:title='data:newerPageTitle'>
          <data:newerPageTitle/>
```

```
          </a>
        </span>
      </b:if>
      <b:if cond='data:olderPageUrl'>
        <span id='blog-pager-older-link'>
          <a class='blog-pager-older-link' expr:href='data:olderPageUrl'
expr:id='data:widget.instanceId + &quot;_blog-pager-older-link&quot;'
expr:title='data:olderPageTitle'>
              <data:olderPageTitle/>
          </a>
        </span>
      </b:if>
      <a class='home-link' expr:href='data:blog.homepageUrl'>
        <data:homeMsg/>
      </a>
      <b:if cond='data:mobileLinkUrl'>
        <div class='blog-mobile-link'>
          <a expr:href='data:mobileLinkUrl'>
            <data:mobileLinkMsg/>
          </a>
        </div>
      </b:if>
    </div>
    <div class='clear'/>
  </b:includable>
  <b:includable id='post' var='post'>
    <div itemscope=" itemtype='http://schema.org/blogPost'>
      <b:if cond='data:post.firstImageUrl'>
        <meta expr:content='data:post.firstImageUrl' itemprop='url'/>
      </b:if>
      <h1 class='post-title entry-title' itemprop='name'>
        <b:if cond='data:post.link'>
          <a expr:href='data:post.link'>
            <data:post.title/>
          </a>
        <b:else/>
        <b:if cond='data:post.url'>
          <b:if cond='data:blog.url != data:post.url'>
            <a expr:href='data:post.url'>
              <data:post.title/>
            </a>
            <b:else/>
            <data:post.title/>
          </b:if>
```

```
            <b:else/>
            <data:post.title/>
          </b:if>
        </b:if>
      </h1>
      <div class='post-header'>
        <div class='post-header-line-1'>
          <span class='post-comment-link'>
            <b:if cond='data:blog.pageType != &quot;item&quot;'>
              <b:if cond='data:blog.pageType != &quot;static_page&quot;'>
                <b:if cond='data:post.allowComments'>
                  <b:include data='post' name='comment_count_picker'/>
                </b:if>
              </b:if>
            </b:if>
          </span>
        </div>
        <span class='post-timestamp'>
          <b:if cond='data:top.showTimestamp'>
          Please rate us | Post Reviews
          <br/>
          <span class='wE' id='13937370307976'>
            <script src='http://widget-
engine.com/w:0:003:13937370307976:6:000:40' type='text/javascript'>
            </script>
          </span>
          <data:top.timestampLabel/>
          <b:if cond='data:post.url'>
            <meta expr:content='data:post.canonicalUrl' itemprop='url'/>
            <a class='timestamp-link' expr:href='data:post.url' rel='bookmark'
title='permanent link'>
              <abbr class='published' expr:title='data:post.timestampISO8601'
itemprop='datePublished'>
                <data:post.timestamp/>
              </abbr>
            </a>
            <span class='post-author vcard'>
              <b:if cond='data:top.showAuthor'>
                <b:if cond='data:post.authorProfileUrl'>
                  <span class='fn' itemprop='author'>
                    <meta expr:content='data:post.authorProfileUrl'
itemprop='url'/>
                    <a expr:href='data:post.authorProfileUrl' rel='author'
title='author profile'>
```

```
            <span itemprop='name'>
              <data:post.author/>
            </span>
          </a>
        </span>
        <b:else/>
        <span class='fn' itemprop='author'>
          <meta expr:content='data:post.authorProfileUrl'
itemprop='url'/>

          <a expr:href='data:post.authorProfileUrl' rel='author'
title='author profile'>

            <span itemprop='name'>
              <data:post.author/>
            </span>
          </a>
        </span>
      </b:if>
    </b:if>
  </span>
    </b:if>
  </b:if>
  </span>
  </div>
  </div>
  <b:if cond='data:blog.metaDescription == &quot;&quot;'>
  <!-- Then use the post body as the schema.org description,
for good G+/FB snippeting. -->
  <div class='post-body entry-content' expr:id='&quot;post-body-&quot;
+ data:post.id' itemprop='blogPost'>
    <data:post.body/>
    <div style='clear: both;'/>
    <!-- clear for photos floats -->
  </div>
  <b:else/>
  <div class='post-body entry-content' expr:id='&quot;post-body-&quot;
+ data:post.id' itemprop='blogPost'>
    <data:post.body/>
    <div style='clear: both;'/>
    <!-- clear for photos floats -->
  </div>
  </b:if>
  <b:if cond='data:post.hasJumpLink'>
    <div class='jump-link'>
```

```
                <a expr:href='data:post.url + &quot;#more&quot;'
expr:title='data:post.title'>
                    <data:post.jumpText/>
                </a>
                </div>
            </b:if>
            <div class='post-footer'>
              <div class='post-footer-line post-footer-line-1'>
                <span class='post-author vcard'>
                  <b:if cond='data:top.showAuthor'>
                    <b:if cond='data:post.authorProfileUrl'>
                      <span class='fn' itemprop='author'>
                        <meta expr:content='data:post.authorProfileUrl'
itemprop='url'/>
                        <a expr:href='data:post.authorProfileUrl' rel='author'
title='author profile'>
                          <span itemprop='name'>
                            <data:post.author/>
                          </span>
                        </a>
                      </span>
                      <b:else/>
                      <span class='fn' itemprop='author'>
                        <meta expr:content='data:post.authorProfileUrl'
itemprop='url'/>
                        <a expr:href='data:post.authorProfileUrl' rel='author'
title='author profile'>
                          <span itemprop='name'>
                            <data:post.author/>
                          </span>
                        </a>
                      </span>
                    </b:if>
                  </b:if>
                </span>
                <span class='post-timestamp'>
                  <b:if cond='data:top.showTimestamp'>
                    <data:top.timestampLabel/>
                    <b:if cond='data:post.url'>
                      <meta expr:content='data:post.canonicalUrl' itemprop='url'/>
                      <a class='timestamp-link' expr:href='data:post.url' rel='bookmark'
title='permanent link'>
                        <abbr class='published' expr:title='data:post.timestampISO8601'
itemprop='datePublished'>
```

```
              <data:post.timestamp/>
            </abbr>
          </a>
        </b:if>
      </b:if>
    </span>
    <span class='post-comment-link'>
      <b:if cond='data:blog.pageType != &quot;item&quot;'>
        <b:if cond='data:blog.pageType != &quot;static_page&quot;'>
          <b:if cond='data:post.allowComments'>
            <b:include data='post' name='comment_count_picker'/>
          </b:if>
        </b:if>
      </b:if>
    </span>
  </div>
</div>
</b:includable>
<b:includable id='postQuickEdit' var='post'>
  <b:if cond='data:post.editUrl'>
    <span expr:class='&quot;item-control &quot; + data:post.adminClass'>
      <a expr:href='data:post.editUrl' expr:title='data:top.editPostMsg'>
        <img alt='' class='icon-action' height='18'
src='http://img2.blogblog.com/img/icon18_edit_allbkg.gif' width='18'/>
      </a>
    </span>
  </b:if>
</b:includable>
<b:includable id='shareButtons' var='post'>
  <b:if cond='data:top.showEmailButton'>
    <a class='goog-inline-block share-button sb-email'
expr:href='data:post.sharePostUrl + &quot;&amp;target=email&quot;'
expr:title='data:top.emailThisMsg' target='_blank'>
        <span class='share-button-link-text'>
          <data:top.emailThisMsg/>
        </span>
    </a>
  </b:if>
  <b:if cond='data:top.showBlogThisButton'>
    <a class='goog-inline-block share-button sb-blog'
expr:href='data:post.sharePostUrl + &quot;&amp;target=blog&quot;'
expr:onclick='&quot;window.open(this.href, \&quot;_blank\&quot;,
\&quot;height=270,width=475\&quot;); return false;&quot;'
expr:title='data:top.blogThisMsg' target='_blank'>
```

```
          <span class='share-button-link-text'>
            <data:top.blogThisMsg/>
          </span>
        </a>
      </b:if>
      <b:if cond='data:top.showTwitterButton'>
        <a class='goog-inline-block share-button sb-twitter'
expr:href='data:post.sharePostUrl + &quot;&amp;target=twitter&quot;'
expr:title='data:top.shareToTwitterMsg' target='_blank'>
          <span class='share-button-link-text'>
            <data:top.shareToTwitterMsg/>
          </span>
        </a>
      </b:if>
      <b:if cond='data:top.showFacebookButton'>
        <a class='goog-inline-block share-button sb-facebook'
expr:href='data:post.sharePostUrl + &quot;&amp;target=facebook&quot;'
expr:onclick='&quot;window.open(this.href, \&quot;_blank\&quot;,
\&quot;height=430,width=640\&quot;); return false;&quot;'
expr:title='data:top.shareToFacebookMsg' target='_blank'>
          <span class='share-button-link-text'>
            <data:top.shareToFacebookMsg/>
          </span>
        </a>
      </b:if>
      <b:if cond='data:top.showOrkutButton'>
        <a class='goog-inline-block share-button sb-orkut'
expr:href='data:post.sharePostUrl + &quot;&amp;target=orkut&quot;'
expr:title='data:top.shareToOrkutMsg' target='_blank'>
          <span class='share-button-link-text'>
            <data:top.shareToOrkutMsg/>
          </span>
        </a>
      </b:if>
      <b:if cond='data:top.showPinterestButton'>
        <a class='goog-inline-block share-button sb-pinterest'
expr:href='data:post.sharePostUrl + &quot;&amp;target=pinterest&quot;'
expr:title='data:top.shareToPinterestMsg' target='_blank'>
          <span class='share-button-link-text'>
            <data:top.shareToPinterestMsg/>
          </span>
        </a>
      </b:if>
    </b:includable>
```

```
<b:includable id='status-message'>
  <b:if cond='data:navMessage'>
    <div class='status-msg-wrap'>
      <div class='status-msg-body'>
        <data:navMessage/>
      </div>
      <div class='status-msg-border'>
        <div class='status-msg-bg'>
          <div class='status-msg-hidden'>
            <data:navMessage/>
          </div>
        </div>
      </div>
    </div>
    <div style='clear: both;'/>
  </b:if>
</b:includable>
<b:includable id='threaded-comment-form' var='post'>
  <div class='comment-form'>
    <a name='comment-form'/>
    <b:if cond='data:mobile'>
      <p>
        <data:blogCommentMessage/>
      </p>
      <data:blogTeamBlogMessage/>
      <a expr:href='data:post.commentFormIframeSrc' id='comment-editor-
src'/>
      <iframe allowtransparency='true' class='blogger-iframe-colorize
blogger-comment-from-post' frameborder='0' height='410' id='comment-editor'
name='comment-editor' src='' style='display: none' width='100%'/>
      <b:else/>
      <p>
        <data:blogCommentMessage/>
      </p>
      <data:blogTeamBlogMessage/>
      <a expr:href='data:post.commentFormIframeSrc' id='comment-editor-
src'/>
      <iframe allowtransparency='true' class='blogger-iframe-colorize
blogger-comment-from-post' frameborder='0' height='410' id='comment-editor'
name='comment-editor' src='' width='100%'/>
    </b:if>
    <data:post.friendConnectJs/>
    <data:post.cmtfpIframe/>
    <script type='text/javascript'>
```

```
                BLOG_CMT_createIframe(&#39;<data:post.appRpcRelayPath/>&#39;,
&#39;<data:post.communityId/>&#39;);
            </script>
          </div>
        </b:includable>
        <b:includable id='threaded_comment_js' var='post'>
  <script async='async' expr:src='data:post.commentSrc' type='text/javascript'/>

  <script type='text/javascript'>
    (function() {
      var items = <data:post.commentJso/>;
      var msgs = <data:post.commentMsgs/>;
      var config = <data:post.commentConfig/>;

// <![CDATA[
      var cursor = null;
      if (items && items.length > 0) {
        cursor = parseInt(items[items.length - 1].timestamp) + 1;
      }

      var bodyFromEntry = function(entry) {
        if (entry.gd$extendedProperty) {
          for (var k in entry.gd$extendedProperty) {
            if (entry.gd$extendedProperty[k].name == 'blogger.contentRemoved') {
              return '<span class="deleted-comment">' + entry.content.$t + '</span>';
            }
          }
        }
        return entry.content.$t;
      }

      var parse = function(data) {
        cursor = null;
        var comments = [];
        if (data && data.feed && data.feed.entry) {
          for (var i = 0, entry; entry = data.feed.entry[i]; i++) {
            var comment = {};
            // comment ID, parsed out of the original id format
            var id = /blog-(\d+).post-(\d+)/.exec(entry.id.$t);
            comment.id = id ? id[2] : null;
            comment.body = bodyFromEntry(entry);
            comment.timestamp = Date.parse(entry.published.$t) + ";
            if (entry.author && entry.author.constructor === Array) {
              var auth = entry.author[0];
```

```
      if (auth) {
        comment.author = {
          name: (auth.name ? auth.name.$t : undefined),
          profileUrl: (auth.uri ? auth.uri.$t : undefined),
          avatarUrl: (auth.gd$image ? auth.gd$image.src : undefined)
        };
      }
    }
    if (entry.link) {
      if (entry.link[2]) {
        comment.link = comment.permalink = entry.link[2].href;
      }
      if (entry.link[3]) {
        var pid = /.*comments\/default\/(\d+)\?.*/.exec(entry.link[3].href);
        if (pid && pid[1]) {
          comment.parentId = pid[1];
        }
      }
    }
    comment.deleteclass = 'item-control blog-admin';
    if (entry.gd$extendedProperty) {
      for (var k in entry.gd$extendedProperty) {
        if (entry.gd$extendedProperty[k].name == 'blogger.itemClass') {
          comment.deleteclass += ' ' + entry.gd$extendedProperty[k].value;
        } else if (entry.gd$extendedProperty[k].name == 'blogger.displayTime') {
          comment.displayTime = entry.gd$extendedProperty[k].value;
        }
      }
    }
    comments.push(comment);
  }
}
return comments;
};

var paginator = function(callback) {
  if (hasMore()) {
    var url = config.feed + '?alt=json&v=2&orderby=published&reverse=false&max-results=50';
    if (cursor) {
      url += '&published-min=' + new Date(cursor).toISOString();
    }
    window.bloggercomments = function(data) {
      var parsed = parse(data);
```

```javascript
        cursor = parsed.length < 50 ? null
            : parseInt(parsed[parsed.length - 1].timestamp) + 1
        callback(parsed);
        window.bloggercomments = null;
      }
      url += '&callback=bloggercomments';
      var script = document.createElement('script');
      script.type = 'text/javascript';
      script.src = url;
      document.getElementsByTagName('head')[0].appendChild(script);
    }
  };
  var hasMore = function() {
    return !!cursor;
  };
  var getMeta = function(key, comment) {
    if ('iswriter' == key) {
      var matches = !!comment.author
          && comment.author.name == config.authorName
          && comment.author.profileUrl == config.authorUrl;
      return matches ? 'true' : ";
    } else if ('deletelink' == key) {
      return config.baseUri + '/delete-comment.g?blogID='
          + config.blogId + '&postID=' + comment.id;
    } else if ('deleteclass' == key) {
      return comment.deleteclass;
    }
    return ";
  };

  var replybox = null;
  var replyUrlParts = null;
  var replyParent = undefined;

  var onReply = function(commentId, domId) {
    if (replybox == null) {
      // lazily cache replybox, and adjust to suit this style:
      replybox = document.getElementById('comment-editor');
      if (replybox != null) {
        replybox.height = '250px';
        replybox.style.display = 'block';
        replyUrlParts = replybox.src.split('#');
      }
    }
```

```
    if (replybox && (commentId !== replyParent)) {
      document.getElementById(domId).insertBefore(replybox, null);
      replybox.src = replyUrlParts[0]
          + (commentId ? '&parentID=' + commentId : '')
          + '#' + replyUrlParts[1];
      replyParent = commentId;
    }
  };

  var hash = (window.location.hash || '#').substring(1);
  var startThread, targetComment;
  if (/^comment-form_/.test(hash)) {
    startThread = hash.substring('comment-form_'.length);
  } else if (/^c[0-9]+$/.test(hash)) {
    targetComment = hash.substring(1);
  }

  // Configure commenting API:
  var configJso = {
    'maxDepth': config.maxThreadDepth
  };
  var provider = {
    'id': config.postId,
    'data': items,
    'loadNext': paginator,
    'hasMore': hasMore,
    'getMeta': getMeta,
    'onReply': onReply,
    'rendered': true,
    'initComment': targetComment,
    'initReplyThread': startThread,
    'config': configJso,
    'messages': msgs
  };

  var render = function() {
    if (window.goog && window.goog.comments) {
      var holder = document.getElementById('comment-holder');
      window.goog.comments.render(holder, provider);
    }
  };

  // render now, or queue to render when library loads:
  if (window.goog && window.goog.comments) {
```

```
      render();
    } else {
    window.goog = window.goog || {};
    window.goog.comments = window.goog.comments || {};
    window.goog.comments.loadQueue = window.goog.comments.loadQueue || [];
    window.goog.comments.loadQueue.push(render);
    }
   })();
// ]]>
  </script>
</b:includable>
            <b:includable id='threaded_comments' var='post'>
              <div class='comments' id='comments'>
                <a name='comments'/>
                <h4>
                  <data:post.commentLabelFull/>
                  :
                </h4>
                <div class='comments-content'>
                  <b:if cond='data:post.embedCommentForm'>
                    <b:include data='post' name='threaded_comment_js'/>
                  </b:if>
                  <div id='comment-holder'>
                    <data:post.commentHtml/>
                  </div>
                </div>
                <p class='comment-footer'>
                  <b:if cond='data:post.allowNewComments'>
                    <b:include data='post' name='threaded-comment-form'/>
                    <b:else/>
                    <data:post.noNewCommentsText/>
                  </b:if>
                </p>
                <b:if cond='data:showCmtPopup'>
                  <div id='comment-popup'>
                    <iframe allowtransparency='true' frameborder='0' id='comment-
actions' name='comment-actions' scrolling='no'>
                    </iframe>
                  </div>
                </b:if>
                <div id='backlinks-container'>
                  <div expr:id='data:widget.instanceId + &quot;_backlinks-
container&quot;'>
                      <b:if cond='data:post.showBacklinks'>
```

```
            <b:include data='post' name='backlinks'/>
          </b:if>
        </div>
      </div>
    </div>
  </b:includable>
</b:widget>
<b:widget id='PopularPosts1' locked='false' title='Popular Posts'
type='PopularPosts'>
  <b:includable id='main'>
<b:if cond='data:title'>
  <h1>
    <data:title/>
  </h1>
</b:if>
<div class='widget-content popular-posts'>
  <ul>
    <b:loop values='data:posts' var='post'>
      <li>
        <b:if cond='data:showThumbnails == &quot;false&quot;'>
          <b:if cond='data:showSnippets == &quot;false&quot;'>
          <!-- (1) No snippet/thumbnail -->
          <a expr:href='data:post.href'>
            <data:post.title/>
          </a>
          <b:else/>
          <!-- (2) Show only snippets -->
          <div class='item-title'>
            <a expr:href='data:post.href'>
              <data:post.title/>
            </a>
          </div>
          <div class='item-snippet'>
            <data:post.snippet/>
          </div>
          </b:if>
          <b:else/>
          <b:if cond='data:showSnippets == &quot;false&quot;'>
          <!-- (3) Show only thumbnails -->
          <div class='item-thumbnail-only'>
            <b:if cond='data:post.thumbnail'>
              <div class='item-thumbnail'>
                <a expr:href='data:post.href' target='_blank'>
```

```
                <img alt='Blog Archives - your-blog-URL-here.blogspot.com'
expr:height='data:thumbnailSize' expr:src='data:post.thumbnail'
expr:width='data:thumbnailSize'/>
                </a>
                </div>
              </b:if>
              <div class='item-title'>
                <a expr:href='data:post.href'>
                  <data:post.title/>
                </a>
              </div>
            </div>
            <div style='clear: both;'/>
            <b:else/>
            <!-- (4) Show snippets and thumbnails -->
            <div class='item-content'>
              <b:if cond='data:post.thumbnail'>
                <div class='item-thumbnail'>
                  <a expr:href='data:post.href' target='_blank'>
                    <img alt='Blog Archives - your-blog-URL-here.blogspot.com'
expr:height='data:thumbnailSize' expr:src='data:post.thumbnail'
expr:width='data:thumbnailSize'/>
                  </a>
                </div>
              </b:if>
              <div class='item-title'>
                <a expr:href='data:post.href'>
                  <data:post.title/>
                </a>
              </div>
              <div class='item-snippet'>
                <data:post.snippet/>
              </div>
            </div>
            <div style='clear: both;'/>
          </b:if>
        </b:if>
      </li>
    </b:loop>
  </ul>
</div>
</b:includable>
</b:widget>
</b:section>
```

```
            </div>
          </div>
        </div>
        <!-- end content-wrapper -->
        <div id='sidebar2-wrapper'>
          <b:section class='sidebar2' id='sidebar2' preferred='yes'>
            <b:widget id='CustomSearch1' locked='false' title='Search Popular Posts'
type='CustomSearch'>
              <b:includable id='main'>
                <!-- only display title if it's non-empty -->
                <b:if cond='data:title != &quot;&quot;'>
                  <h2 class='title'>
                    <data:title/>
                  </h2>
                </b:if>
                <div class='widget-content'>
                  <div expr:id='data:widget.instanceId + &quot;_form&quot;'>
                    <span class='cse-status'>
                      <data:loadingMsg/>
                    </span>
                  </div>
                </div>
              </b:includable>
            </b:widget>
            <b:widget id='HTML3' locked='false' title='' type='HTML'>
              <b:includable id='main'>
                <!-- only display title if it's non-empty -->
                <b:if cond='data:title != &quot;&quot;'>
                  <h2 class='title'>
                    <data:title/>
                  </h2>
                </b:if>
                <div class='widget-content'>
                  <data:content/>
                </div>
              </b:includable>
            </b:widget>
            <b:widget id='BlogArchive1' locked='false' title='Blog Archive'
type='BlogArchive'>
              <b:includable id='main'>

                <b:if cond='data:title'>
                  <h2>
                    <data:title/>
```

```
      </h2>
    </b:if>
    <div class='widget-content'>
      <div id='ArchiveList'>
        <div expr:id='data:widget.instanceId + &quot;_ArchiveList&quot;'>
          <b:if cond='data:style == &quot;HIERARCHY&quot;'>
            <b:include data='data' name='interval'/>
          </b:if>
          <b:if cond='data:style == &quot;FLAT&quot;'>
            <b:include data='data' name='flat'/>
          </b:if>
          <b:if cond='data:style == &quot;MENU&quot;'>
            <b:include data='data' name='menu'/>
          </b:if>
        </div>
      </div>
    </div>
  </b:includable>
  <b:includable id='flat' var='data'>
    <ul class='flat'>
      <b:loop values='data:data' var='i'>
        <li class='archivedate'>
          <a expr:href='data:i.url'>
            <data:i.name/>
          </a>
          (
          <data:i.post-count/>
          )
        </li>
      </b:loop>
    </ul>
  </b:includable>
  <b:includable id='interval' var='intervalData'>
    <b:loop values='data:intervalData' var='i'>
      <ul class='hierarchy'>
        <li expr:class='&quot;archivedate &quot; + data:i.expclass'>
          <b:include data='i' name='toggle'/>
          <a class='post-count-link' expr:href='data:i.url'>
            <data:i.name/>
          </a>
          <span class='post-count' dir='ltr'>
            (
            <data:i.post-count/>
            )
```

```
      </span>
      <b:if cond='data:i.data'>
        <b:include data='i.data' name='interval'/>
      </b:if>
      <b:if cond='data:i.posts'>
        <b:include data='i.posts' name='posts'/>
      </b:if>
    </li>
  </ul>
 </b:loop>
</b:includable>
<b:includable id='menu' var='data'>
  <select expr:id='data:widget.instanceId + &quot;_ArchiveMenu&quot;'>
    <option value=''>
      <data:title/>
    </option>
    <b:loop values='data:data' var='i'>
      <option expr:value='data:i.url'>
        <data:i.name/>
        (
        <data:i.post-count/>
        )
      </option>
    </b:loop>
  </select>
</b:includable>
<b:includable id='posts' var='posts'>
  <ul class='posts'>
    <b:loop values='data:posts' var='i'>
      <li>
        <a expr:href='data:i.url'>
          <data:i.title/>
        </a>
      </li>
    </b:loop>
  </ul>
</b:includable>
<b:includable id='toggle' var='interval'>
  <b:if cond='data:interval.toggleId'>
    <b:if cond='data:interval.expclass == &quot;expanded&quot;'>
      <a class='toggle' href='javascript:void(0)'>
        <span class='zippy toggle-open'>
          &#9660; 
        </span>
```

```
      </a>
      <b:else/>
      <a class='toggle' href='javascript:void(0)'>
        <span class='zippy'>
          <b:if cond='data:blog.languageDirection == &quot;rtl&quot;'>
            &#9668; 
            <b:else/>
            &#9658; 
          </b:if>
        </span>
      </a>
    </b:if>
  </b:if>
    </b:includable>
  </b:widget>
  <b:widget id='HTML10' locked='false' title='Blogspot Templates' type='HTML'>
    <b:includable id='main'>
      <!-- only display title if it's non-empty -->
      <b:if cond='data:title != &quot;&quot;'>
        <h2 class='title'>
          <data:title/>
        </h2>
      </b:if>
      <div class='widget-content'>
        <data:content/>
      </div>
    </b:includable>
  </b:widget>
  <b:widget id='HTML1' locked='false' title='' type='HTML'>
    <b:includable id='main'>
      <!-- only display title if it's non-empty -->
      <b:if cond='data:title != &quot;&quot;'>
        <h2 class='title'>
          <data:title/>
        </h2>
      </b:if>
      <div class='widget-content'>
        <data:content/>
      </div>
    </b:includable>
  </b:widget>
  </b:section>
</div>
<div id='footer-wrapper'>
```

```
        <b:section class='footer' id='footer'/>
      </div>
      <div id='credit-wrapper'>
        <div id='link-wrapper'>
<a href='#' target='_top' title=''><span itemprop='url'>Home</span></a> | <a
href='#' target='_blank' title=''>Google Library</a> | <a href='#' target='_blank'
title=''>Case-Gallery</a> | <a href='#' target='_blank' title=''>Free-SEO-Tools</a> |
<a href='#' target='_blank' title=''>Advanced-Search</a>
          <br/>
          Copyright(c)2014-2017
          <br/>
          <a href='http://tina-andrew.blogspot.com/' target='_blank'>
            tina andrew
          </a>
          <br/>
          Back to
          <a href='#go-top'>
            TOP^
          </a>
        </div>
      </div>
    </div>
  </div>
  </body>
</HTML>
```

-------------------------------- oooOooo --------------------------------

Blogspot Template Designer for Validator.w3.org
We try to do our best to serve you better.
Thanks for purchasing this Script and please feedback here:
http://www.facebook.com/dev7cyber2012

Best Regards,
Template Designer,

Herman Nz
Lampung - Indonesia